NOV 3 1979

The Seals

by
Iona Seibert Hiser

Illustrated by Nancy McGowan

Steck-Vaughn Company
An Intext *Publisher*
Austin, Texas

Front Cover: Ribbon, or Banded, Seal
Center: Walrus

Back Cover: (top) Harp Seal
(bottom) Fur Seal

Stellar Sea Lions

Library of Congress Cataloging in Publication Data
Hiser, Iona Seibert.
  The Seals.
  (Steck-Vaughn wildlife series)
  SUMMARY: Discusses the characteristics, habits, and endangered species of sea lions, fur seals, walruses, and true seals.
  1. Pinnepedia—Juvenile literature. [1. Seals (Animals) 2. Walruses. 3. Sea lions] I. McGowan, Nancy, illus. II. Title.
QL737.P6H57   599'.745   74-13584
ISBN 0-8114-7768-1

ISBN 0-8114-7768-1
Library of Congress Catalog Card Number 74-13584
Copyright © 1975 by Steck-Vaughn Company, Austin, Texas
All Rights Reserved
Printed and Bound in the United States of America

Seals

Basking in the sun on the cobblestone beach of a coastal island is a colony of seals. The animals watch as a small boat approaches. Suddenly, many of the seals lunge down an incline. Barking, roaring, and yelping fill the air. Then the curious creatures, playfully and with amazing swiftness, swim out to meet their human visitors.

These seals are sea lions. They, as well as many other kinds of seals, live along some of the coasts of all the continents of the world.

A World of Seals

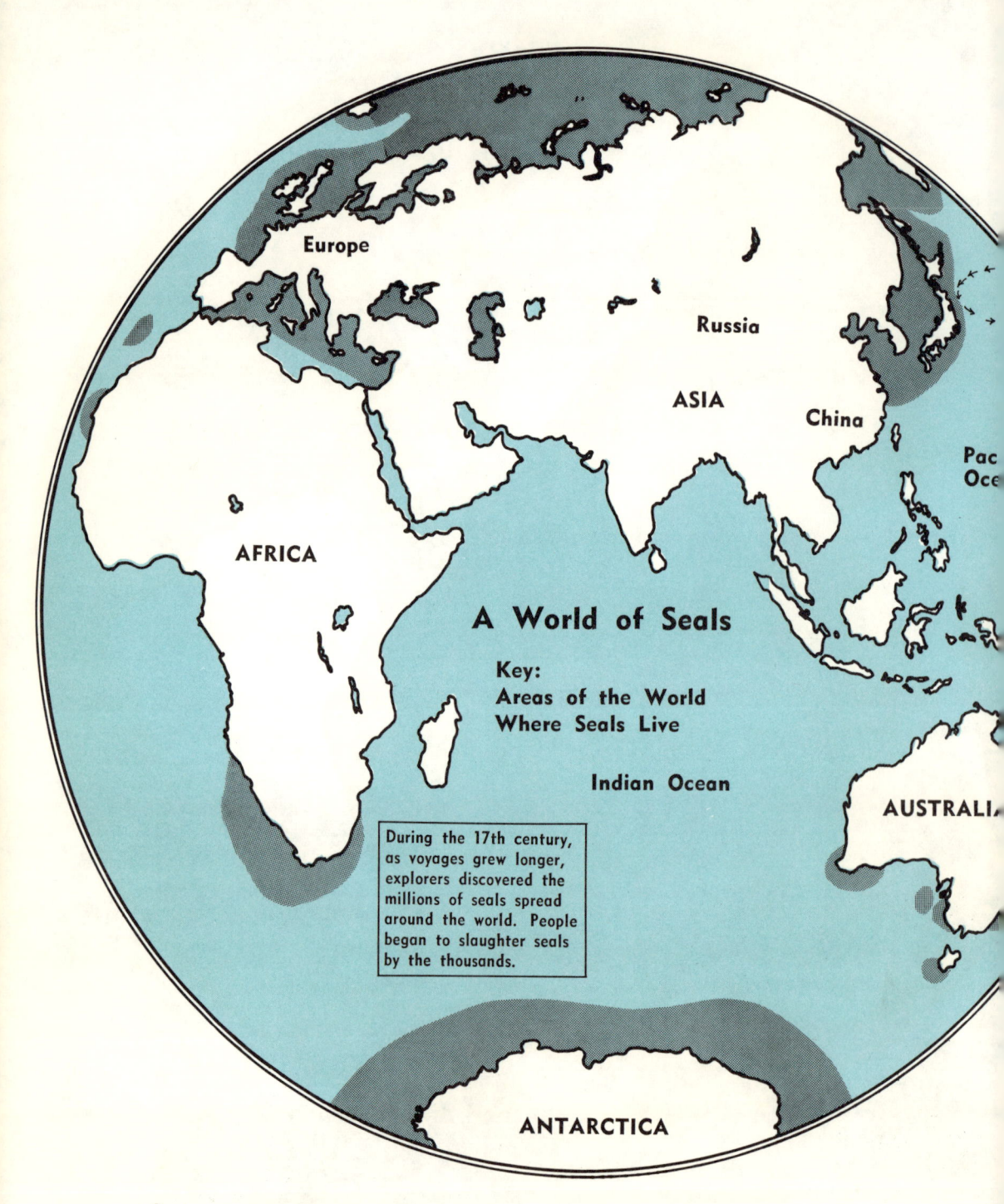

Key:
Areas of the World Where Seals Live

Europe
Russia
ASIA
China
AFRICA
Pac Oce
Indian Ocean
AUSTRALIA
ANTARCTICA

During the 17th century, as voyages grew longer, explorers discovered the millions of seals spread around the world. People began to slaughter seals by the thousands.

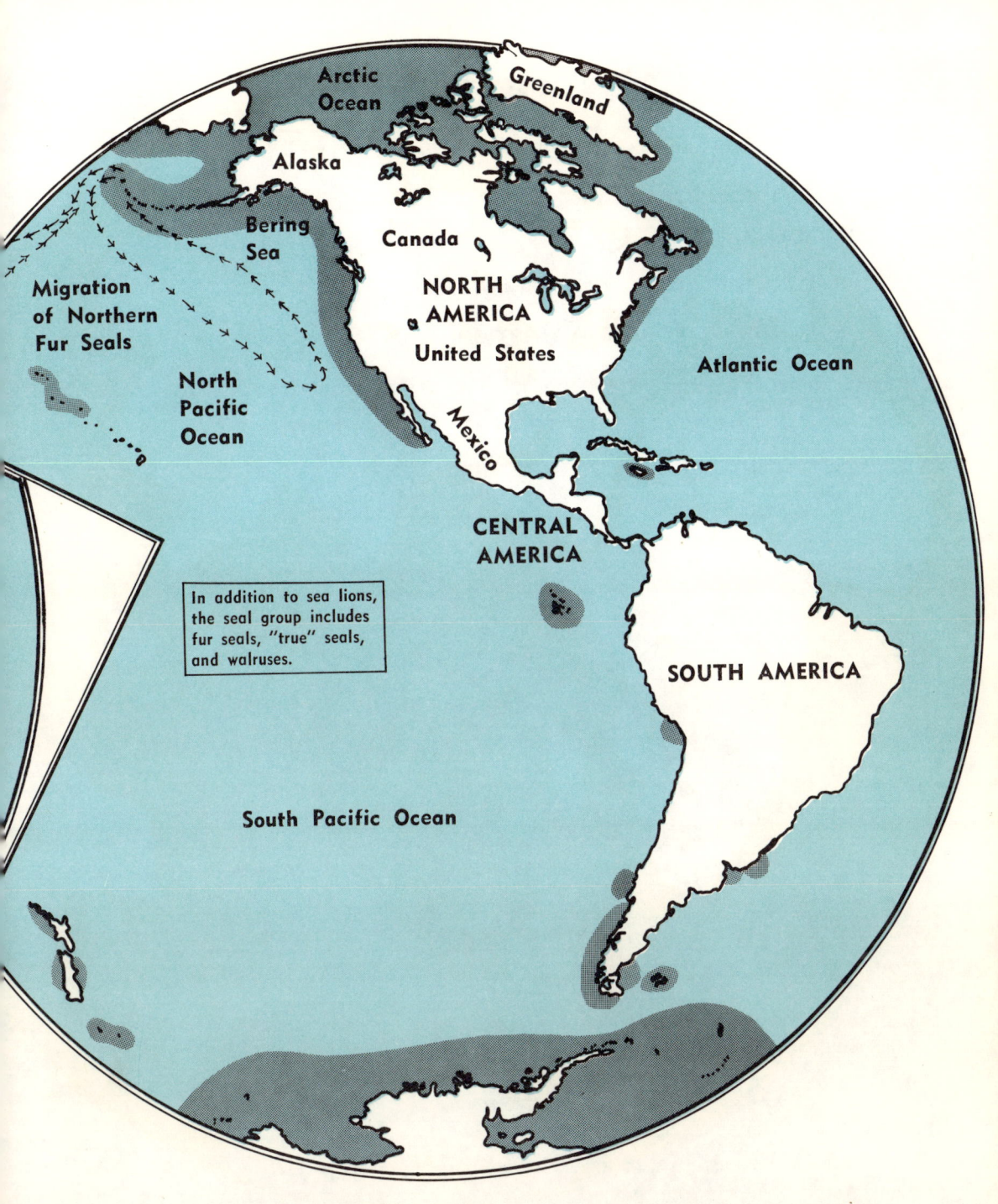

Arctic Ocean
Greenland
Alaska
Bering Sea
Canada
NORTH AMERICA
United States
Mexico
Atlantic Ocean
Migration of Northern Fur Seals
North Pacific Ocean
CENTRAL AMERICA
SOUTH AMERICA
South Pacific Ocean

In addition to sea lions, the seal group includes fur seals, "true" seals, and walruses.

Classification of Seals

Seals are aquatic (uh-qua-tic), or water-living, mammals. The 31 species (spee-sheez), or kinds, of seals are grouped together in the Order Pinnipedia (pin-i-pee-dee-uh), meaning fin-footed. They are often called "pinnipeds."

Pinnipeds are related to the family of animals containing dogs, bears, and weasels.

Mammals are animals that have hair on their bodies and give birth to living young.

Female Gray Seal with Pup

Characteristics of All Seals

Good Sight and Good Hearing
(in and out of water)
Streamlined Body
Layer of Blubber
Hair or Fur

— Rear Flippers

In size, seals range from the small Baikal seal, about 4½ feet long, that lives in Siberia, to the huge elephant seals, 16 to 20 feet long and weighing 5,000 to 8,000 pounds.

Front Flippers

External Ear Flaps or Ear Openings

Large Brown Eyes (adults)

Whiskers
Teeth

Common, or Harbor, Seal

Development of the Pinnipeds

Many millions of years ago the ancestors of seals lived only on land. They walked on 4 well-developed legs. But as the ages progressed, the group of animals that was to develop, or evolve, into the pinnipeds, spent more and more time in the water. Gradually, over a long period of time, their bodies became more pointed and streamlined. Limbs shortened and finally withdrew into the bodies. Toes became part of a webbing that resembled birds' wings. Eventually, the feet became flippers, or fins, that were useful for swimming.

Pinnipedia, or members of the seal order, with flippers have existed for about 20,000,000 years.

During the time of developing, some species lost their external ears but retained the hair and fur of their primitive ancestors.

Habits

Although aquatic, seals have retained a liking for land. They pick secluded spots along seacoasts to come ashore. These areas are called "hauling out" places. Such sites are also known as "rookeries," and the herd of animals is sometimes called a "rookery," especially during the breeding season.

Some seals stay at sea for weeks, sometimes for many months. They even rest and sleep in the water. But all pinnipeds need land at times. Land is essential for finding mates and having pups.

Baikal Seals

Some species of seals live in lakes and rivers.

Pinnipeds can travel far out to sea. California sea lions have been seen feeding 39 miles from shore. Seals that live in fresh water are found far inland at times.

Seals are graceful swimmers and divers. Some species can descend to a depth of more than 1000 feet in the sea. Their nostrils close tightly when they dive. Pinnipeds can stay submerged for several minutes. Some species can stay under water 20 or 40 minutes.

**Northern Fur Seal
(Sleeping)**

Species that live continuously in the sea for months have various ways of sleeping and resting. Some float on their backs. Others float upright with heads out of the water. But some have been observed to sleep submerged, coming up occasionally for air.

Mature Male Elephant Seal

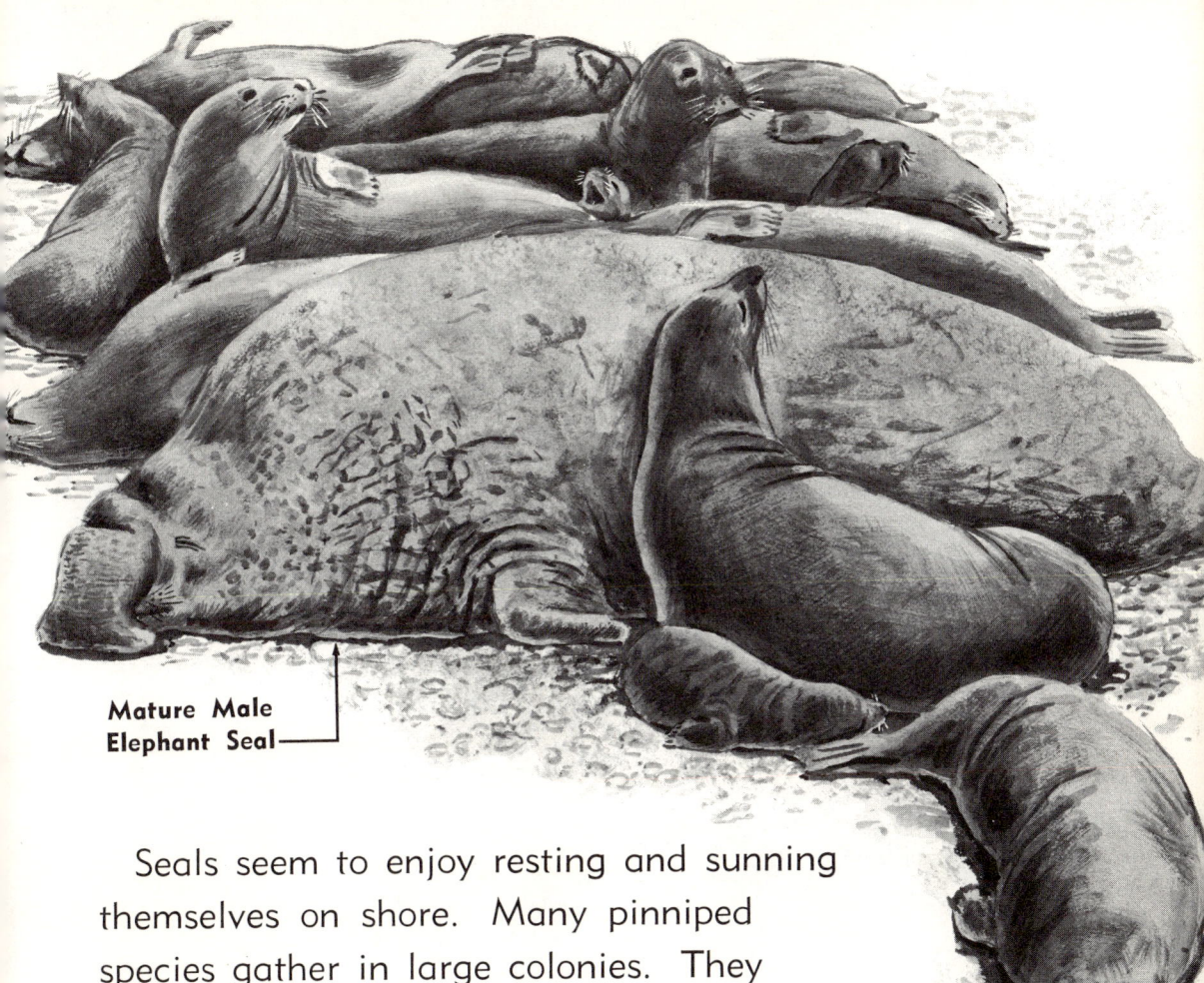

Elephant seals especially like to crowd close together in very compact groups.

Seals seem to enjoy resting and sunning themselves on shore. Many pinniped species gather in large colonies. They may choose rocky or sandy beaches. Others prefer to propel themselves out of the water onto high rocks or ice floes.

Some seal species are very sociable. They lie in such compact groups they often pile on top of each other. This frequently ends in tragedy, for many newborn pups are crushed and killed and adults may be injured.

Protection from Cold

Seals are warm-blooded animals that can adjust to various temperatures. They can live in both cold and temperate climates. Hair and fur help to insulate their bodies. Under their tough skin is a thick layer of fat called "blubber" which gives further protection against cold. Their skin contains glands which secrete oil that covers skin and hair and helps to "waterproof" the animals.

Weddell Seals

Protection from Heat

To help rid themselves of surplus body heat, seals pant and wave their flippers. They may flip sand over their bodies for protection from heat. But seals may become so overheated after exertion on land that they can die from heat exhaustion.

Alaskan Fur Seals

Southern Sea Lions

Reproduction

Mating seasons differ with the species and the habitat, or home, of the animals. Some seals form harems, or groups of females. Bulls, the male seals, often arrive first at the rookeries to choose territories. In species that have harems, the dominant bull chooses as many mates as he wants and fights off the other males. The losers then live on the outskirts of the rookery.

Seal pups are born about a year after mating occurs. The fertilized egg is usually carried in the seal cow's body for months before developing.

The young are nursed for only a short time—from a few weeks to several months. A seal mother has very rich milk, and the cubs of most species grow amazingly fast. They are soon ready for life at sea.

Many seal pups are born with blue eyes. But the eyes change to brown as the seal matures. Hair color varies and usually is woolly and wavy. Pups of the gray, ringed, and harbor seals are born with pretty white hair coats. Fur seal, elephant seal, and sea lion pups arrive with dark wavy hair.

Harp Seal Pup

Elephant Seal Pup

What Various Seals Like To Eat

Penguin

Shrimp

Cod

Herring

Squid

Sea Lion
The species, such as sea lions and fur seals, that feed on fish have better developed teeth than those that feed on invertebrates (in-<u>ver</u>-tuh-brates), animals without backbones.

Rockfish

Crab

Lamprey

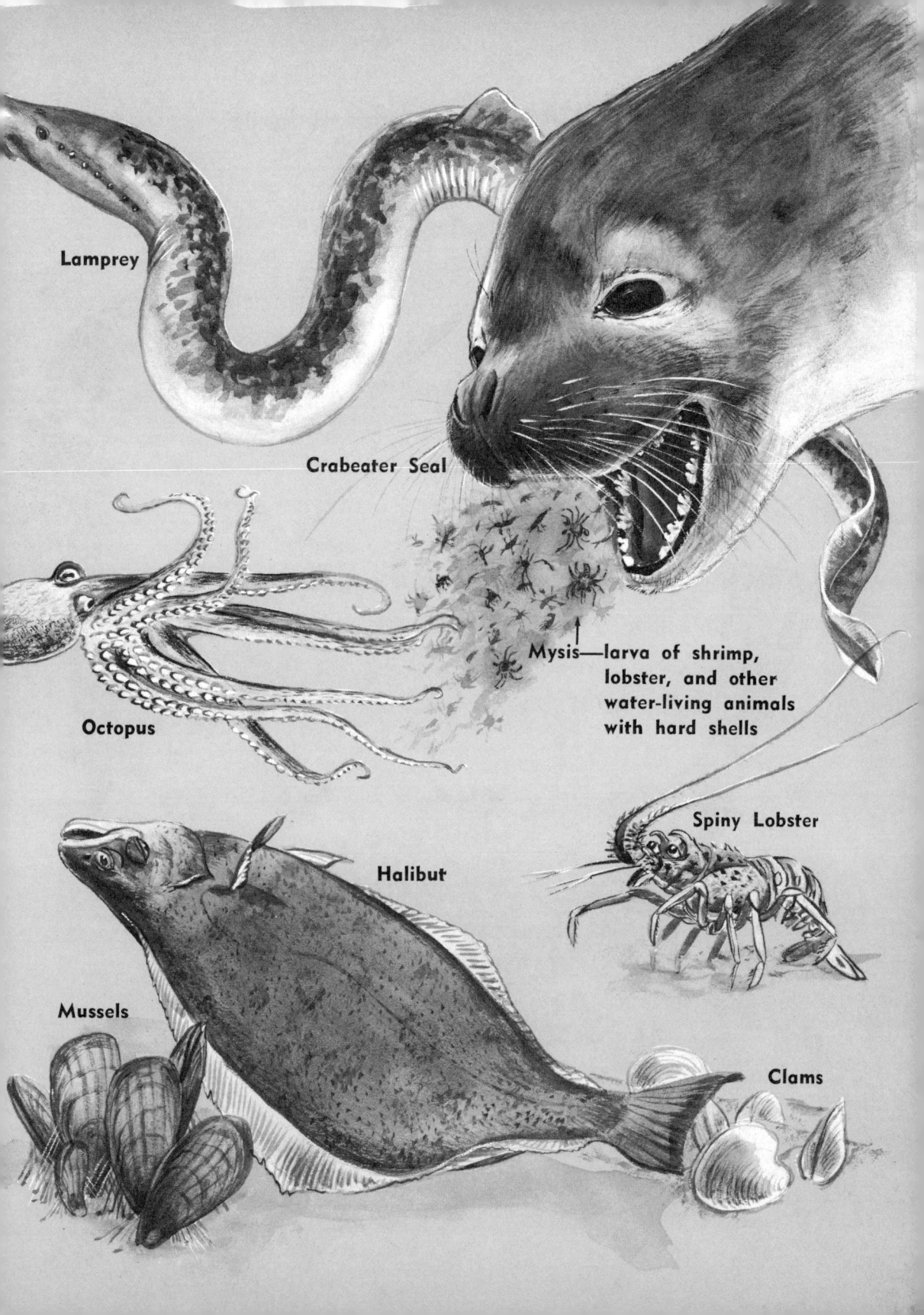

Crabeater Seal

Octopus

Mysis—larva of shrimp, lobster, and other water-living animals with hard shells

Spiny Lobster

Halibut

Mussels

Clams

The Three Families of Seals

The different kinds of pinnipeds are placed in three groups—sea lions and fur seals, walruses, and the true seals.

The Otariidae (o-tuh-rye-uh-dee) Family contains sea lions and the fur seals. Seals in this family have external ears. Since the hind flippers can be turned forward, sea lions and fur seals can walk on all fours and can move rapidly on land. The soles of the flippers are hairless, leatherlike, and smooth. To swim, these animals use only the fore flippers. Hind flippers are used like a rudder on a boat.

California Sea Lions

Sea lions are often seen in small groups quite far from land, romping through the water, leaping in and out. Sea lions travel so fast it is difficult for the human eye to keep track of them.

Sea lions are the most playful of all the pinnipeds. They chase fish and play with seaweed and air bubbles. Like other seals, they have mock battles. Sea lions are also skilled surf riders. California sea lions are well known for their many tricks and are the trained seals of animal shows.

Fur Seals

Of the fur seals, the northern species is the most famous. These seals were hunted almost to extinction for their fur hides. But controlled hunting and scientific study have rescued the northern fur seal. It is no longer considered an endangered species.

Guadalupe Fur Seals

Pup **Female** **Male**

The Guadalupe fur seal was once killed in such vast numbers along the California coast that the species was almost gone by the twentieth century. From 1928 through 1949 this fur seal was considered extinct. Then a small herd was discovered on Guadalupe Island off the coast of Mexico. Today, the United States Department of the Interior includes the Guadalupe fur seal on the Threatened Mammal list. The mammals on this list are few in numbers or are in danger of becoming extinct.

Walruses

The Odobenidae (o-doe-ben-i-dee) Family contains only the walruses. These arctic seals have long upper canine (kay-nine) teeth, or tusks. The ivory tusks gave them their scientific name, Odobenidae, which means "he who walks with his teeth." The tusks help walruses haul themselves out of water or move over rocks on land.

The tusks of old males sometimes reach a length of 3½ feet. Tusks of the Pacific Ocean species are longer and more bowed than tusks of the Atlantic Ocean species. Both species are now found only in the Arctic Circle.

Female Walrus

Walrus mothers nurse their young much longer than other seal species. The walrus pups live on mother's milk for about two years, until their tusks have grown long enough to dig for their own adult food, clams, from the bottom of the ocean.

Young Walrus

Except for a little wrinkle in the skin, walruses have no outer ears.

The walrus uses its bushy mustache with hundreds of movable stiff bristles to help push food into its mouth. The tusks are used to dig clams, a favorite food, from the bottom of the sea.

On land or aboard an ice floe, the walrus herd posts a guard. If danger is sighted, the guard sends forth a peculiar bellow, warning the others to flee for safety into the sea.

Male walruses sometimes reach a length of 12 feet and weigh up to 3,000 pounds.

Like members of the Otariidae Family, walruses use all four flippers for land travel. It has been reported that the walrus will chase a careless hunter and that the animal can run as fast as a man. Walruses have been known to attack boats, using their big tusks to gouge and slash, even hooking the tusks over the boat's side to capsize it.

When swimming, walruses use their front flippers as paddles while swinging the rear end of their bodies from side to side.

When walruses migrate either north or south, they often ride drifting ice floes. But when a herd is swimming, the pups often ride on the mothers' backs.

The True Seals

The Phocidae (foe-suh-dee) Family is made up of about 15 species of the true seals. These animals have no external ear flaps. Their hair-covered hind flippers are turned backwards permanently and cannot be used for walking. The true seals travel on shore awkwardly, but with a flowing muscular movement of their bodies. Hind flippers are seen trailing along behind or uplifted in the air.

Seals in the Phocidae Family swim with a side-to-side motion of hind flippers and the rear end of the body.

Hooded Seals

The hooded, or bladdernose, seal of the North Atlantic and Arctic Ocean has an air sac on top of its head which can be inflated to form a hood sometimes larger than a football.

Some of the True Seals

Harbor, or common, seals are found throughout the Northern Hemisphere. These seals sometimes live in freshwater lakes, as well as in salt water. Liking the land, they spend much time on smooth sandy beaches. If disturbed, the animals take to the water. Later, they float back slowly to cautiously look over the situation. If not satisfied that it is safe to come ashore, the seals sink quietly in the water like a submarine.

Harbor Seal

The Antarctic leopard seal's spotted throat probably gave the animal its name. This seal has a reputation for viciousness and preys upon the young of other seals.

Elephant seals are the largest of the Phocidae. The mature male's nose, the proboscis, looks like an elephant's trunk. The proboscis can be inflated. The mature male of the northern species can inflate the proboscis and blow down into the open mouth to make a loud sound. The noise, resounding from the mouth cavity, is a harsh, rhythmic pounding that is a challenge to other bulls.

Elephant Seal

Natural Enemies of Seals

Polar Bear

**Two Ringed Seals
(Surrounded by Enemies)**

Leopard Seal

**Gramus
(Killer Whale)**

Great White Shark

25

Endangered Seals

Hawaiian Monk Seal

Mediterranean Monk Seal

Caribbean Monk Seal

Seals in Danger!

In addition to the Guadalupe fur seal, three other species of seals are placed on the list of Threatened Mammals of the United States: the ribbon seal, the Caribbean monk seal, and the Hawaiian monk seal.

The ribbon, or banded, seal lives in the North Pacific Ocean, between the continents of Asia and North America. Little is known about this rare seal.

The Caribbean monk seal, formerly found on the shores and islands of the Caribbean Sea and Gulf of Mexico, may be extinct. In 1494, Columbus and his men sighted these animals sleeping on the sands of south Haiti. They called the seals "sea wolves."

The Hawaiian monk seal now has a safe home in the Hawaiian Islands National Wildlife Refuge. Like the other threatened species, this seal was once slaughtered by the thousands.

Ribbon Seal

A Walrus Carving

Seals and People

Primitive peoples had to kill seals. They depended upon the animals for food. All parts of the seals were needed.

But later, people killed for greed. A great sealing industry developed during the 17th century. Sealskin coats and muffs became fashionable. Oil from seal blubber was used for heat and light. Walrus teeth were prized for their ivory.

The killing of seals during their seasonal migrations at sea by commercial hunters prevented breeding. The numbers of seals began to be greatly reduced.

Concerned nations made laws to control seal hunting. In 1911, and again in 1957, treaties between nations stopped the slaughter of seals at sea. In 1972, the Marine Mammal Protection Act was passed by the United States Congress. This law prohibits the killing of marine mammals except by special permission.

But seals are still threatened. People have invaded remote beaches and frightened seals away from their natural habitat. Seals suffer from the pollution of the oceans, part of their environment (en-vi-ruhn-ment). And the slaughter of seals may still continue in some areas.

If nations will work together to regulate seal hunting and protect the natural habitats, perhaps the seals can be saved.

The world of seals is also the world of humans. What affects the food and water of one also affects the other. Survival of the seals may be our survival, too!

Steck-Vaughn Wildlife Series

Concerned with the appreciation and conservation of wildlife, the Series presents information about endangered species and animals of the southwest.

The American Buffalo, Wanda L. Pearson
The Armadillo, Theodore W. Munch and M. Vere DeVault
The Bighorn Sheep, Iona S. Hiser
The Black-Footed Ferret, J. M. Roever
The Brown Pelican, J. M. Roever
Collared Peccary—The Javelina, Iona S. Hiser
The Coyote, Iona S. Hiser
The Gila Monster, Iona S. Hiser
The Grizzly Bear, Sibyl Hancock
Horned Lizards, M. Vere DeVault and Theodore W. Munch
The Mountain Lion, Iona S. Hiser
The Mustangs, J. M. Roever and Wilfried Roever
The North American Alligator, Jim Pruitt and Nancy McGowan
The North American Eagles, J. M. Roever and Wilfried Roever
The Pronghorn, Iona S. Hiser
The Road Runner, Theodore W. Munch and M. Vere DeVault
The Southern Sea Otter, Ernie M. Holyer
The Western Diamondback Rattlesnake, Evelyn M. Brown and M. Vere DeVault
The Whooping Crane, J. M. Roever
Wolves, J. M. Roever